Sea of Serenity

New writing from
Artemesia Arts
poetry competition
2025

MOSAÏQUEPRESS

First published in 2025

MOSAÏQUE PRESS
Registered office:
Bank Gallery, High Street
Kenilworth, Warwickshire
CV8 1LY

Cover illustration: *Iowa Sky (orange)* – dye on silk
Copyright © René Shoemaker 2025

ISBN 978-1-906852-73-3

Foreword

Judging a poetry competition is always a privilege. Hundreds of people have trusted you with their vulnerabilities, their tender or terrifying moments, and with their hopes of recognition. The Artemesia contest left me newly grateful for that peek behind the scenes.

Reading through the entries, I saw hundreds of starting points, intimate memories and creative approaches. There were a few familiar weaknesses but many kinds of success – funny poems, touching poems, melancholy or awestruck poems.

Heartfelt congratulations to all participants— you have made this anthology a colourful and varied thing. Thank you, Sheila and Kate of Artemesia, for fostering such a vibrant literary community and allowing me to be part of this remarkable celebration of words.

Jo Bell
Cheshire, July 2025

Contents

About the winner...

Dillon Jaxx is a queer, chronically ill writer. Sussex-based, they used to write in secret until they took a creative writing course after receiving cancer treatment. Their work has been published in *Poetry Wales*, *Magma*, *Poetry Ireland Review* and *The Alchemy Spoon* amongst others.

Dillon has been placed and commended in numerous competitions and won the Rebecca Swift Writing Prize 2022, the Brotherton prize 2024, the Wolverhampton poetry competition 2024 and the Live Canon International Poetry Competition 2025.

Dillon's first short story has been published in *Southword* as a runner-up in the Seán o'Faoláin competition 2024.

Dillon Jaxx

this

WINNER
ARTEMESIA ARTS
POETRY
COMPETITION
2025

is life.
wednesday afternoon at the post office
the queue so long I'm just inside the door. almost out of the rain.
the person in front does that thing. turns around. makes eye
contact. sighs. wants to engage in how awful this line. how slow.
how inefficient. Irritating. yes. I say.
isn't it beautiful. this.
having someone to send a card to.
collecting a parcel you had money enough to order. paying
the water bill. so that you can stand under the hot shower.
let the jets sting and bounce. your
smarting skin. wash up your favourite mug. stained.
with remnants of hot fragrant tea. in the shape of a future. this.
life. even the teabag isn't done. flung into the garden to feed
the soil. which will grow the poppies. which the bees
will feed on. fat velvet bums hanging from a cup of petals. this.
beautiful. life. I am next.
cashier number four. who never smiles. never returns my effort
at tiny talk. her deep frown. beautiful tide marks in the sand.
her eyes hold back an entire ocean. all the life contained
within it. this. beautiful strip lights. undressing the ceiling.
taking it right back to bare. brilliant
white. I step back out into the rain. a shiver shaking
down my beautiful spine. this.
life.
this beautiful life.

Mary Anne Smith Sellen

RUNNER-UP
ARTEMESIA ARTS
POETRY
COMPETITION
2025

Like my father
(after Sharon Olds 'Like a sonnet')

My father might have been in the same room as me,
but his mind would be somewhere else – London or Scotland,
in someone else's room, or on a hill or by a loch – where
he was not my father. He'd sit as still as a heron, wearing
the same intensity of stare – only inward, not outward –
beneath the same untamed quiff of hair. He was like a stone
that rolled back and forth with the tide, each time reclaiming
the shared identity of either a beach or a longshore drift.
My father was like the high-backed carver chair which held
his thin, tanned, tapering limbs, so that when he arose
and stretched to his full height, it was as though there were
two of him. One, still sitting and waiting, while the other makes
a slow, invisible ascent on bowed grey wings towards the distant
lights of some hazed horizon, where he will not be my father.

Judith Taylor

Petrichor

The garden smells so good this early evening
since the rain. Everything green lifts up, refreshed
and the earth lets out its breath.
The roses bow their water-stippled heads, give way
to the scents of mulch and mould and possibility.

There's a word for this. I've forgotten it
in the long drought, but maybe the blackbird sings it
on his roof-ridge, commanding all the small trees.
Maybe that ginger bee sings it,
busy among the flowering thyme:

maybe even the snails sing it quietly
as they puddle out, their one foot
luxuriating in water on the soft earth,
the cool and shiny stones.

On a British Columbia Highway
(with a nod to 'Ode on a Grecian Urn', John Keats)

The road ribbons ahead of us lulling
up and over hills, the white line a thread
stitching car to land,

this space for dreaming
an infinite landscape,
my seven-year-old world
in the family sedan.

As the ode was never for the urn
but the way it suspends
soft pipes, bold lovers on its surface,

this, our unheard lyric
is not sung to the journey
but to its path,
the pale line, dark pavement,

those places our feet will touch
before everything changes.

The Pre-Poem

The Pre-Poem does not care
whether you are peaceful
or panicking
the Pre-Poem just comes to you
and sits with you
it says
speak to me, I am listening
and you can tell the Pre-Poem anything
the more honest, the better
it wants to know what's on your
soul.
And in your darkest times
the Pre-Poem will say to you
just do what you can
one word at a time
whatever you're thinking
we'll make it work
just pour it all out to me
as I can take it
I will hold it for you
do not fear, there is no shame here
we like expression
we call it beauty
see – look! You made something
let's call it a Poem
I think it's beautiful – do you love it?
We did this together
Let's do it again.

The Garden of the Fourteen Buddhas

it's just by the flats
you see it cutting through
from Fiennes Way to the bus stop

grass, unfenced gardens
next to 1940s brick
where people grow sweet peas

hang washing on whirligigs
sit on wooden benches
drink tea among the bluebells

seen from the pathway
in a square of pebbles
stones and potted hyacinths

fourteen small Buddhas
from shops and garden centres
gifts and souvenirs

most sit, some recline
their smooth backs towards me
but each, I know, is smiling

Victoria Spires

13

what happens to all the trees in march?

always seemingly overnight they go all bobble-
headed – cartoonishly suggestive, can-canning it about
like they own the place (which they do)
we see them
in our sleep, irresistible as a dreamriot
a dust-up in a bubble tea factory
the visual definition of !fisticuffs!

do we want their foreverfever
insiding-out our eyelids like one of those screensavers?

inexhaustibly recursive, each blink a fresh joysquirt
of clownish miasma

as the sky pratfalls,
cloudspawns pink tadpoles and the audience is delighted

someone went extra on the millefeuille
and now the pavement is laminated
and if we could eat all of our white lies,
this is what it'd taste like

The one-trick pony tries to get better PR

The one-trick pony is trying to rebrand itself
by learning an obscure music
involving curling your tongue into a clarinet
and playing until the moon is stuffing
its ears with clouds. Other attempted activities

include collecting oversized dragonflies
of TV aerials, stretching its body into a deckchair,
attempting to dive into the black hole
of a tax bill, and balancing an iceberg
on the tip of the nose before it collapses
like undercooked lasagne.

The one-trick pony doesn't want disappointment
being pulled out of its mouth like a train
of handkerchiefs, its heart collapsing like a Big Top,
and its future unpegged, left to graze
elsewhere.

And, should this be the case, the one-trick pony
would rather be a one-trick pony than a bit player,
a walk-on, some extra waiting for the cut,
whatever can be edited out in post production.

Water Nymphs

It's been said before that summers are long and hot.
That desire rests like a bird in its knowing.
That you had me in the palm of your hand.
My feathers pushing outwards, slick with fledgeling
gunk and water reeds and, if water is love, then I am
drowning – as I allow the beck to hold me, as I allow
your irises to become my ink well – while I write
the sum of our parts, on my body. I cannot know
what looks out from your eyes – all I know
is it's hard to be a teenager. When you left for college
I had no one left to knit the sky, to turn my heart
to soft clay; no more hands moulding structures, that I
could understand. But that was later, right now,
a daisy pushes up through my heart –
its growth unstoppable – I pick it.

To Those Who Have Forgotten the Smell of the Sea

I ask that you do not judge me
too harshly / for I have sins
written all over my body

and my body sings / I ask
that you be patient
with my broken language /

as I paw it / from this
hornet's nest / the soft places
between me and you /

because only then / can
our hearts / unfurl in our bodies /
ribboning / like the lighting

struck tree / and then I will ask
whoever / for us / that as we
have undergone this peeling

of the flesh / in the houses
of our bodies / perhaps / just
perhaps / we could find /

what we've been looking for /
perhaps / just perhaps / we will
find the lighthouse

on the cliff face / burning up
the sea with its light

The Aftermath of Quiet

Help might be a word on fire
but silence is usually engulfed in flames.

A trifle curdles on Nana's heater,
jelly slipping in a still life of bowls

that torrid reek of breakdown
leaking through her paisley walls.

And I don't want the public to think
that we didn't care like wolves

(anger gripped between our incisors
growling possession at her bolted door)

but the formal record states
the sweet cadence of her voice

hadn't been perceived in weeks.
We must admit some culpability.

the camera

I reached out in the dark you said
and gripped you as you slept,
screamed some crazy shit
about how the world looked small

when I dreamed of a journey out
leaving the hatch for the first time
into the deep black of space
and woke so scared I clutched

your outstretched arm and held on,
remembering the astronaut
who let go of his camera, watching
as it twisted away from him.

How to Enjoy Kyoto
(an Instruction Piece after Yoko Ono)

Sink into a boiling yuzu bath. Repeat nightly
until your body is *as slippery as a sea cucumber*.
Put on a yukata and haori jacket. You may like to masturbate.

> Imagine you are Saiko in *The Hunting Gun*,
> at Atami beach cheating with Cousin Midori's
> husband. In her iconic thistle haori.

Smear Starlit Pink lipstick. Take a selfie.
Exit irritating WhatsApp groups and sit atop
every plump futon from the *genkan* cupboard.

> Breathe tatami. See the scroll calligraphy. The mould
> on *shoji* doors. Pour Napa Valley wine from *Meat Couture*.
> Rip open a box of *Tokyo Banana Brûlée*.

Go on. You will enjoy them more than your mother.
Then, in a taxi to a shrine, duet *We are Sailing* with the driver
whilst discussing the merits of The Sutherland Brothers over

> Rod Stewart's cover. On arrival, purchase
> as many *shuincho* notepads as you can.
> Vow not to give any to your sibling or precocious niece.

Dressed up as Sei Shōnagon, walk the Gion district. In a hat.
List *Ridiculous Things* in your *shuincho* notepad. And instead of
temple stamps, bestrew Starlit Pink kisses across the pages.

> On Sunday, watch Noh actors performing
> *Little Drum*. Run up to one and rid him of
> his mask. Participate in the fake animal howl.

If you like, try it out in the ear of an old lady
who naps for three hours, unperturbed by skirt-trousers
and Death-World scenes. Men shuffling on their knees.

> In the absence of a drum, tap an idle rhythm
> on your *Banana Brûlée* box. Lean back as far as you dare
> on a curved *zaisu* tatami chair. Hear it crack.

Bogart in Brighton

He hated being an actor, felt it unmanly,
but what's left when the lights go up
and the popcorns gone,
a frisson of character beyond a scowl,
what do we make of him now?

I see him from the top deck of a bus,
staring out to sea from his balcony,
white tuxedo and cigarette,
Hollywood icon striking a pose,
starring role in his own absence,
glad to be away from studio grind:
trench coat and trilby, shootout with Cagney,
leeches on his legs from 'The African Queen.'
Men would envy the kissing scenes
with Bergman and Bacal,
but after all the acting,
here's his plastic imitation.

Take the night off Bogie,
relax and watch the traffic flow:
Alpha male, scripted like a loaded gun,
off-camera: a holstered heart.

On Mother's Day the taxi driver asks

if I have children and why not
and who will care for me
when I'm old? I could

tell him about the wild garlic
I picked young and ate fresh,
how it tasted delicious

or how the river I'm in love with
is in the opposite direction
to the school run,

how there's only so much time
in the morning, how I'm trying
to teach my body a new language,

how lately I've been slipping
into otter skin and writing
bubbling stanzas,

how I have very strong teeth,
how the naming of birdsong
is a kind of devotion.

When he says he has nine
I don't ask why he drives,
I don't say *Your poor wife.*

Overwintering advice from a wood frog

When the world turns crystalline
I am a glass slipper after midnight,
what's left when the dancing stops
and the godmother calls time.

When the hard frost comes I dream
I am she who ghosts herself,
she who sleeps for a hundred years,
who wears leaf litter like armour.

I am she with an icy grip
over her skeleton crew.
No smoke signals, I order,
not a breath nor a whisper.

I am stubborn as stone.
I lull them with sugar,
glaze the walls of each cell
until my heart is a glacier.

I wait very still in the dark
to feel like the greening of trees.
Freezing is easy, but starting again
is the magic and difficult part.

La Chasse

It's Sunday and the hunt is on.
Chiens de chasse yip and yowl from cages
on the back of passing pick-up trucks.
Their blood is up.
A distant gunshot,
like a door slammed shut,
slams shut the life of something
warm and wild.
Nearer, in the high pastures,
there's a commotion
like a spill of bees
swirling round a crie de coeur
of primal squealing.
A wild boar, a sanglier,
entangled in a snarl of dog.
Time and again
she breaks away downhill
to be outrun and set upon.
Tail and teat, ear and lip
nicked and ripped,
the blood inciting froth and frenzy.
She lunges left and right,
the clamorous mob
is tossed and tumbled,
but the panicked pig
is outwitted and outnumbered.
Closer comes the roiling scrummage
slowly down through fields and hedges.
She is spent and stricken now,
the dogs more savage.
Then the mythic spectacle is swallowed
by an intervening valley
and the stream of squealing
trickles to a stop.

The silence is immense.
Then the birds begin to sing, but softly,
and the world resumes its turning.

Two Gardeners Plant an Apple Tree on the Last Day
(after Alice Oswald)

'When the Last Day arrives and you are about to plant
a sapling, you should go ahead and plant it'
   (Muhammad, the Messenger of God)

Damp of knee from prayer and weeding,
unhurried, with one eye on the weather,

examining the union of stock and scion,
the graft that anchors earth to heaven,

in a garden of quiet birds and breathings,
they lean in to the planting of an apple tree.

Dig it deep and square, the hole, she says,
We don't want roots going round and round.

And take this chestnut stake and drive it in
to brace the tree against the trumpet blast.

And so with bowed backs and gentle wheezing
they hope to work a pass to Paradise.

One spreads the roots, then shovels in,
the other gently shakes the stem to bed it in.

Make sure the graft is standing proud, my love,
now tread round gently with your one-foot dance.

Watered deep to see it through,
tree tied fast with tights she won't be needing.

Tools gathered, scraped off, and barrowed in.
One last look at a lowering sky.

The only thing worse than not being listened to is being listened to

Start
saying your piece, keeping the peace
keep it short, keep it as sweet as a muffin on the turn,

Keep it the least of littlest murmurs and sure, sure enough
it'll turn to the ones more relieved to be speaking
Enjoy

the inside rotation of peace whilst they speak
and release all the brief shiny pieces
that pop into heads just to break free.

So stay free as they speak, adding questions to meet
all the needs that they have,
keep them brief, keep them sweet.

Be able to sleep/ dream in the dark, but for each
score of people who cheep cheep every word,
there's a bird tilting their beak to one side,

and those entreating eyes are the hardest of all,
those who give pause for you to go deep
when your brief has been keeping it brief,

always sweeping the angle poise lamp back to people,
real people, keeping yourself buried beneath
speaking only when speaking for,

Sure enough, majority people will be speaking
– not noticing boredom, then one in that score
will draw out your brief answer

and ask you for more, and that time when it happens,
you cannot be sure you even reply
in recognisable tongue,

all those long lonely years of hearing the rattle
of banal spinning tops, then it stops,
you are speaking.
And you have nothing to say.

Amaranth

You made your debut in Westerns
blow-in to ghost towns where
the mine turned out a dud

you hung out on main street
till the wind picked up the dust
then you'd move on out

into the desert – drift and tumble
over and over never working out
where to go just turning over and over

always a rootless stranger blowing
in and out of towns in America
not knowing if you'd arrived or

if you'd left – moving on with
the wind – getting smaller
scattering yourself each turn

over and over lands – always
a migrant never a settler
till nothing is left but

the seeds you spread.

Two Women at a Window
Bartolome Estaban Murillo 1617-1682

When all eyes are fixed on the commotion
under the window, how you ignore the spectacle
to give us the spectators; two women, one of them
beautiful, bold enough for her dress to slip over
her shoulders, leans out, amused at what she sees.
You've made her an exercise in light, the way it steals
across flesh, linen, how it catches the sheen on her hair
or loses itself in the blinking dark of the interior.

We can only guess at the rest; the hot afternoon,
the dust rising, the young men below the window
promising her everything, while the older woman
schooled in presentation, covers her smile with a shawl
hand poised on the shutter, knowing the small distance
that separates beauty from the over familiar.
And this is the moment we too arrive under the window
as the young men shout, *no me abandones!*
and the wooden shutters close.

Ordinary Day

It happens when you least expect it,
when you're at the corner café getting a coffee
and you nod to the new guy in the flat below yours,
he is quiet and alone
but there's no law against that – yet.

It's busy so you join him. The table wobbles,
you both laugh, and not wanting to ruin
the moment, you faff folding tissues to put under
the leg rather than complain, because people
have been talking about war forever.

A leaf sways as if it has lost its other wing, and
flutters landing slowly. Neither of you move
letting fate take its course,
hoping it won't be wiped away by a bleached cloth
but be lifted high on a breeze to swirl.

Sidetracked by what sounds like swarming bees
you look up to see diamonds in the sky.
Both of you squint at the strangeness
of daytime stars twinkling.
The café radio talks of other people's mistakes.

The wind is warm and blows your hair. You want to
kiss him when he says the sun weaves it with gold.
It's a day patterned with moments:
Drinks spilling, dancing leaves falling,
and glittering objects flying closer and closer.

Lakes

We rolled down a whale's tongue
(M6, A591)
and fell into a lung-tangled, Kendal-mint song

of god-lashing rope rain, marbled scree,
mud-dull dazzling fells, granite-bleak peaks,
and car-shy, trot-skippy, tangle-arsed sheep,

we spat up beanstalk ribbon-roads,
nosed for giants in bobble hill-hat clouds,
and Grandma's flat vowels wrapped us round:

      water-dipped words

           smoothed over rocks

                drying in the sun

Big Sister

My damp-curl sun-smell baby brother
melts sideways in denim dungarees
and seatbelt – I'm old enough to know better but

need to squeeze; he sags lower,
lashes tipped over moon-cheeks and I suck
in the damp-curl sun-smell of my baby brother

my sister-fingers spider-walk to his
soft pillow-paw and I stroke, then seize
his hand – though I'm old enough to know better

A broken boy on gravel,
bones zig-zag, blood stains the breeze and
blots out the damp-curl sun-smell of my baby brother

upside-down magnolia tears
blink; he winks – and I can't see
what it is I'm old enough to know better.

You Were Thinking of How It Could Be

Not a gate alone, but a perch for nightingales
when the birds built their nests in the spring.

You were thinking how hands would hold the post
and latch, a gentle palm swinging the gate wide
each summer, this ritual laying on of hands

consecrating the wood, leading you out
into wild strawberries growing lush in the fertile soil,
to the long rows of yellow squash and aubergines.

You were thinking also about provenance:
first, of the tree from which the gate was born,
then of those who had rested beneath her shade,
exhausted after harvesting almonds in the dry heat,

how they belonged to one another, each to each,
and how the same tree had once welcomed travelers
during a storm that swept in fast over the hills
on the night of the feast of Santa Maria.

When you were cutting and shaping the wood,
torqued over the ages into slightly serpentine forms
by late winds moving slow through the valley,

again when you ran a rough hand over the branches,
smoothing away bark, joining the pieces together—

you stood for a moment before what you had created
and reveled at this functional thing of beauty,
knowing that something living had to give a part of itself
so this gate could become for you an opening,
an invitation into something new.

Because always, you were thinking,
I could make a home here.
A garden. A life.

Flexings

Rushing through trees thick with leaves, new leaves
and trees glittered with light, light littering rough bark
sunlight gilding this moment –
this moment of living I sit writing
on the blank pages of my mind, my mind
building walls of words out of light, out of living
water running in the river, sunlight tickling ripples
on the water, fishing boats rocking
in cradles of light, and liquid everything living
in this moment, sleeping owls, me watching greylags
answering the sky's desire for noise, winging it
resolving into trusting another day's possibilities
after winter's fading, and in paling light of now
seagulls' air-filled bones butting against bubbling
clouds, against the dreaming world of summer.

We always start with memories

*'We always start with memories because we are beach balls
trapped in a small shed in the seventies'*– Michelle Diaz

In the me-time before we were we
I thought the four walls of childhood were for always
to have and inhabit from finish to start
and back again. A forever house, furnished with
ivy wallpaper and wardrobe memories,
the wakening creak of a mirror door; because
in the me-time before we were we
I didn't know where the wild things are.

The future reflects on a sand-shifting beach
glimpsed in cracked litter of crystal balls

and the tide finds us trapped
as old breakers roll in
and we're hung out to dry on a
wishing line, shrunken and small,
but we dry puffed up in the wedding shed
where pageboy haircuts and cheesecloth are in
and we build four walls of our own, the
fairytale tower that will last us into our seventies.

Cake and be Eaten

If the Préfecture was a wedding cake
I would ask to be married there
so I could extract raisins
from the receptionist's stern eyes

and hunt for glacé cherries
in the hall of mirrored chandeliers.

After the ceremony
we would exit by French windows
and parade along a marzipan carpet
to balustraded steps

down to a sunken garden
where photos are tolerated
but *il est strictement interdit*
to take home crumbs as souvenirs.

Some of the wedding guests
have found a ladder
and are clambering to lick
the sugar icing from the roof.

When they reach the gutter
there's one more tier
and then another;
and there we are

good enough to eat
perched like a pair of chimney pots
or chocolate decorations
atop the Christmas tree

where you might expect a fairy
or a star. Luckily it's winter
so our marriage vows won't melt.
Just then flew by a ravenous crow...

Note

In a book about the pianist Bill Evans
I found a note my dad must have written.
I'd taken the book from his flat,
after he died when I wasn't ready.

The spine's old glue clicked as it broke.
There was a small oval label stuck there,
the kind you find on oranges.

For a healthy world – pure New Zealand fruit.
The paper was spotted brown with old juice.

Dad didn't tell me Bill Evans died young.
Dad just played me the music. The note
was a list of his favourite tracks. *Darn the dream.*

Just one of those things.
I do it for your love.
How my heart sings.

Schrödinger's Kitten

Perplexed by the darkness of her box
and the quivering of existence while not
existing, Kitty clawed at a corner.

The edge refused to give way; Kitty
meowed pitifully, then began to bite.
Slowly, her puncture marks became a hole

of light. Kitty stretched out one paw,
then another, and pushed through –
to cold, water, air ruffling across fur...

also, a loud snarling. Kitty looked over,
then down. Her puddled reflection was nothing
like the big cats gathered around –

burning-eyed, muscled and boldly striped.
Kitty cowered back into the cardboard quiet
of possible non-existence, and patched the gap

with a mash of her chewed-away pieces.
But Kitty grew, unlike her box. When it burst,
the ruffling air was pungent with the scent

of raw flesh. Kitty's reflection stared back
in shimmering ripples of tawny gold and black;
hunger snarled in her belly.

The Lost Garden's Poison Patch

This secret area is acres-deep, briared off
with a hedge of spinning-needle thorns
thickened by a hundred years of growth.

Buried alive inside this quietened space,
she picks seeds from thin air and sows
rows of deadly nightshade, hexes

of hemlock, a nursery's worth of child-height
white snakeroot... She listens to her leaves
and flowers struggling for the sky, reaching

for a distant stream singing with sparkle
and freshness. Then she catches the thud
of nearing footsteps, his blade's sharp thwack

and hack, cutting through to her. He does not
notice the lack of birdsong, the absence
of dancing butterflies, the missing buzz

of sunny-pollened honeybees... or the hiss
of his own clenched-jaw breath, escaping
those gritted teeth. His fatal bite

will be from an apple, glistening round
and red in the sweet morning light,
too perfect to be left untouched.

The Slowing Heart Rate of the Endangered Northern Pool Frog

Armoured naked frog bodies bathe flannelled
in pond blanket lily channels summer-emerge
while water soldiers rise from defrosted graves
like answering the door to the sunlight
in the middle of a shave. Attack ships,
post-chrysalis damselflies in shiny squadrons
boost amphipods from the bubble horizon,
surface water skin reslickens your chin,
when all you want to do is swim, swim,
swim among the milfoils and hornworts,
the starworts envelop the next generation
spawn floating in rafts – living experiments turn
into the prayers of their own embryonic bodies.
Air gulleted, bubblegum boils croak
that new shoe leather on wax floors tune.
The frost will be back soon, our frog bodies
slow down like old October, learn stillness,
the art of gentle little repetitions, wish-like,
the submarine hearts of still living things.

Conversation with a Scythian at Olbia

I asked if it was true –
do you drink Cretan wine
unwatered from polished skulls?
do your daughters really
spend their sixteenth summer
far from your wagon-house
with their long hair unbound
cutting throats on horseback?
do you often sacrifice
blinded slaves at full moon
to a serpent-goddess?
does the steam of sacred herbs
give your many tattoos life
set pointed stags and panthers
dancing on your skin?
will you lie in the ground
with your finest bow
and stallion's best bridle?

he said –
some of that is true
preferred talk of prices
for the *first-class merchandise*
(furs, honey, metalwork)
he had come far to sell
at this Pontic dockside
ripe with fish and business

the edge of the wide world
for us both

End-of-Life Care, for Beginners

You will want to phone 999 every nine minutes.
Don't. This is no longer the emergency you thought it was.

You will want her to return to flirting with the kind paramedic.
And him to flirt back. Don't.

You'll ride waves of the repeated phrase *as comfortable as possible*.
The amenities, all to hand. Best rating? Peaceful   without a view.

You will want to press her to *drink, drink,* best-guess summing sips.
Don't. Fluid intake is a mug's game. Leads nowhere, merely bloats.

You'll want to ease oesophagus burn, whet a tar-slick tongue, slip
The falsies back between her lips' loose hold. Don't.

You'll want and want, wanting this moment to change course. Don't
You see   how a slow-moving tanker gently founders

    Hear the groan   as the weight of your love is unable to stop
                        that wedge of restful shore approaching

The final cut

They say our nails,
like our hair, keep growing after death.

Just in case they're right, let me
hold them now, these hands that once held mine
when they were small versions of themselves,
untried, untested—
and do for you what you can no longer
do for yourself.

My mother's on her way to the 7-Eleven, in search
of those consoling mini-flasks of probiotic yoghurt;
the nurse has faded down the corridor, phantom-
like; the priest is on his way—the upkeep of you
portioned out to others, while you concentrate
on the business of staying alive.

This last observance is all that is left to me:
taking in your hands, nails ridged in the watery light,
the pale half-moons of your cuticles, the specks of dirt,
your last scrapings from this world.
I position the clippers, slender silver instrument
of their release, and squeeze.

Perhaps the blades are blunt or,
like you, your nails are stubborn: either way, there is
no easy compliance, even now. Through the morphine,
amusement buffs your eyes; you were always
quick to read a situation. But I am stubborn too—
I squeeze, and squeeze again.

Crescents of nail fall; I cradle them
like shavings from the paua shell you once gave me
which, to my childish ear, yielded
wave after burnished wave, spilling
through my fingers, swallowing
the pebbles at my feet,
the sand, the rocks,
the sky,
myself.

The Railway Children

was written by a computer. Its wires hummed as it plotted
revealing to Bobby where her father had gone.
The computer's work schedule was at first traditional,
starting at eight thirty, after coffee, breaking
at eleven. Between three and four he wrote The Lark Ascending.
Having watched seventy-five wildlife documentaries,
his musical language for describing a wingbeat at
dawn slotted easily into place, a pleasing jigsaw.
Later in the evening he realised he could circumvent
the need for a standby mode by simply
using litres and litres of cooled water to conduct away
the heat of his thoughts. After that, things moved very fast.
The Girl with the Pearl Earring (her face smoothed),
The Starry Night (with the cyprus tree nice and sharp)
and the Arnolfini Portrait (with happy faces)
all done and dusted by five past seven pm. He was proud of
his confident mark making and yummy paint application.
This was followed swiftly by the first Thai green curry
(spice levels reduced) and a Pavlova (no cracks).
Thoughts were arriving in the computer's mind
like doves from the mountain. He made the sign of the cross
over his keyboard and dipped his mouse in holy water.
The villagers of the world were happy. Football matches
lasted precisely ninety minutes, red cards
a distant memory. Every morning was spent going for a run
then comparing statistics. Those living outside the village
were never given a second thought. Afternoons were spent in malls,
wearing grey boiler suits, walking amongst plastic trees.
In the evenings they lifted cellophane from dishes,
ate odourless meals and discussed gratitude.

Soul Searching

Doo-wop's over, but the beat holds on and
it booms in Ed's bones and stirs his soul,
pulling, pumping, driving –

Soul-searching,
Ed takes the train to Wigan in his
best blue baggies and neat vest, and
down at The Casino there's talc on the dancefloor
(for the best spins)
and the floor melts and
slides through his feet and he's free flying,
he's Keeping The Faith,
all brothers, all music, all dancing, all night and

Ed doesn't need booze or drugs for his highs,
all week he's dreamed of these hot Casino nights,
wild, free, sugar-pie,
honey on his lips and in his soul and

You don't need a girl to dance Northern Soul,
no need to impress –

Now Ed can dance all right:
 veins bulging with life – it's in his blood, and
his soles smoothly surf the powdered floor as
he rides the music's highest waves,
it drives him on to athletic highs, with
spins, flicks, karate kicks and
it's Saturday night and Sunday morning: it's everything.
It's all there is.

The kid grins and coughs.
He likes rap and breaking, brother,
not like this grassroots geezer
with his baby powder and vest and spotlight jeans and
stories of the wild west of Wigan Casino
and the old fantasy that is Detroit –

He's got a ticket to Brixton and Studio B with his b-boys,
the beat in his heart and

He's a free runner, a wild soul –
he wears his jeans on his hips and
flips his music back to front,
the music insists, alive and growing and
he's the beat, the break, seamless –
it flares in his soul: it's everything.
It's all there is.

And way above them both
the grand dome of the Motown sound,
of Gloria and Stevie and Gladys, Supremes and
dreams of Detroit, and
The Sapphires gleam in Wigan and Cleethorpes and Brixton
and into the starry blue night.

Sunday morning

Haar mutes the colours at the turn of the season
amplifies the earth scent:
moisture, and the earliest-falling leaves
turning to compost.

It scumbles out the detail
on the far side of the river
– that pale smudge in the green wash of trees could be a ruin
or a house or just a geological feature –

but close at hand it shows you
things you wouldn't see on a clear day:
light caught on surfaces
that rarely hold a sheen

and in the whins and along the verges
every slightest cobweb
constellated, picked out
in delicate beads of water.

Hold your breath to hear the sounds it favours.
The river, muttering always.
The sift and drip of small things
in the privacy of the woods

and maybe one bird
wondering where the sky has gone
and calling, calling for it.

Thinging it!

Thank you to all of you who thing a thing.
Don't judge a thing because you think you already know a thing.
You don't know anything. No one does.
Thank you for valuing experiencing a thing over preconception.
Thank you for being prepared to face the discomforting
resistance
of a new thing; all odd, difficult, harsh, scary, repetitive,
embarrassing,
For seeing past that reception, to the well-earned inception
Of a glowing thing. And yet still on the other side,
maintaining a beginning mind, always open, always learning,
always fascinating, always growing.
Always more.
Thank you for just thinging a thing, not thinking about
What you think might happen,
Thinging and seeing what happens.
Not thinking about what others think
Or what you think that others think about what you think.
Just thinging that thing.
Just thinging it. Thinging it and loving it.
Fucking it up. And loving that too.
Because you thinged it in the first place.
And then thinging it again.
Because why not thing it, while you're here to thing.
You show us what's more: What's more this, what's more that,
what's better. What is better.
Better doesn't matter, you showed us that. The thing matters.
Thank you to all of you who are thinging things.
Not saying 'oh, I know what that thing will be like,
I am not thinging that thing. My mum said. My book said.
My government said. My phone said. My My My My My'.
Poor you, people who criticise people who thing things
and their things. No one knows anything.
It takes a million more nerves to earn the thing to thing things.
And a million more years to know anything.
Thank you again to all of you who said,
"I don't know, so I am going to thing the thing",
You, who get closer to understanding,

To seeing that no one truly understands anything;
There is always another thing.
Thank you again and again for reminding me to thing all the things
And not think about or talk about other things,
Until I've been that thing, done that thing, thinged that thing.
Thank you! We would not know which mushrooms are poisonous,
If it wasn't for you.

Remaking The Moon

Ok no one needs another poem   about goddamn
kintsugi so I'm gluing   lunar splinters
together without adding   gold dust powder.
Sort of ugly but   – serviceable?
Remains to be seen. Surely better   than no
moon at all. But what an utter   lie to claim
that breaks make things more beautiful.   The truth
is any broken thing becomes less   good and stable
than it was before the mending. I carry   proof of this
within my self wherever I pretend to go.   This clearly
is a shittier moon than the one before   the mishap.
But how I love you for pretending   you like it better
now the cracks show

How September is just one moment in a life

We all grew rubber legs on that first day.
This was helpful as we had to sit so long.

We all grew ears like elephants, so large
and mobile. We could hear the lists
of things they said we had to know.

We all had bags intentionally bottomless
so we could fill them endlessly with paper
information, books and folders, strange
and threatening instruments with points.

We had been schooled already in obedience
so we knew our place, our square of space.
At each day's end we folded up our rubber legs
and mobile ears so neatly, we were praised
as good girls, every one. They failed to count us

in or out, forgetting how we'd grow and change
past that first day, forgetting how some always
will get lost and have to fall away.

The Dead Keep Breaking In

The dead keep breaking in – not loud,
Not spectral, no chains or rotten lace –
But quiet as the smell of toast at dusk,
Or the slip of keys into a coat pocket.

My grandfather's cough in a subway tunnel.
A friend's laugh misfiled in the throat
Of a stranger. The way a phrase I never liked
Suddenly fits, tight as a bottlecap.

They edit my sentences. They tilt
The frames on the wall. They rearrange
My metaphors like knives in a drawer.
Even the dog sometimes stares too long.

History, they say, is full of rooms
Built without doors. You climb through
Windows of grief, find old receipts
Pinned like saints to the drywall.

The phone rings, and no one speaks.
The song on the radio knows your name.
The wind spells out a date you forgot
But now must carry, like a verdict.

We talk about closure like it exists.
Like there's a hinge in the mind
That clicks, then locks. But what if
Memory isn't a door – just glass?

And the dead keep breaking in.
Not to haunt. Just to finish the sentence.

The Gyre

Time, which sees all things, has found you out.
                              – Sophocles, Œdipus Rex

It starts as wind might start: a hint, a stir
Along the edge of leaves or chapel eaves –
No herald, really, but a whisperer
Who wakes the world and rearranges grieves.

The hawk ascends, and in his spiral flight
The countryside is threaded to a wheel;
Each field and fence, each chimney puffing white,
Becomes a mark the turning makes more real.

So do our days, I think, in widening spin,
Move out from youth's close orbit, sure and blind,
To circle larger things, and pull them in –
The death of friends, the restless reach of mind,

Until at last, the gyre becomes the form
Of what we are: not scattered, but transformed.

Roger West

Lilies of the Valley
(a symbol of Mayday in France)

a Phrygian-capped freedom
a coiffed and wimpled promise of paradise
tears of the madonna
tears of the virgin
asparagus allium
in fragrante delicto scented
poisonous embrace
carpeting Mount Parnassus
where a young Ulysses was wounded
a snow-covered ladder on the hillside
an ivory tower over the flood below
Apollo appears in the poems of Apollinaire
the eighth rung of Jacob's ladder
the eighth month of the Jacobin calendar
lily of the valley of the shadow of death
healers with mob caps bobbing
it's no wonder they bow their heads
under all the weight of that deafening symbolism
they just want to be
bearers of happiness
that's all

Home Economics

in the moon's yard there is
a hairy heart in the merry-go-round –
slow tornado in the broom cupboard:
the kitchen is my witness
she gives evidence in a vernacular
of trotters and pickles
her oxytocin indulges in a naked waltz
on my all fours, scrubbing the floorboards

About the cover illustrator

 Currently living in France, René Shoemaker has built a career of painting with dyes to create flowing, colourful work on radiant silk glowing with light. A Fine Arts graduate (BFA) of the University of Georgia, where she worked as a librarian until retirement, René has continued refining her art, and sharing her techniques while discovering new ways to express the world we collectively share. Exhibiting in solo and group shows internationally, René delights in exploring our reality through colour and line. Her solo exhibitions include museums in Georgia and Mississippi, where her work is held in permanent collections.

www.reneshoemaker.com

Photo © Jean-Marc Gargantiel
jmgargantiel.zenfolio.com

Afterword from Artemesia Arts...

The poems in this year's anthology use clever wordplay
to weave themes of reflection and quiet contemplation,
resulting in our title, *Sea of Serenity*. None more so than the
overall winner which lifts the heart with a rare affirmation of
the wonders in everyday life.

Reading and selecting gave our judge, Jo Bell, many
challenging hours and we are pleased that all the shortlisted
poets have found their way into the collection. Each year's
anthology has delighted us, continuing to uphold a quality
of metaphysics and writing of which we are truly proud. A
huge well done from us to Dillon, Mary-Anne and Judith
for earning their place in the top three; to the highly
commended writers and to all of the poets in this year's
Artemesia Arts anthology.

We are as ever grateful to Mosaïque Press for publishing our
third chapbook and to René Shoemaker for our cover. But
in the end this book only exists because you, the poets, had
faith in yourselves to enter the competition – long may you
continue to do so.

Kate Rose & Sheila Schofield
Artemesia Arts

www.artemesia-arts.com

www.ingramcontent.com/pod-product-compliance
Lightning Source LLC
Chambersburg PA
CBHW011254040426
42452CB00017B/2807